Aztec Warriors

by Marc Clint

BELLWETHER MEDIA · MINNEAPOLIS, MN

TM

Are you ready to take it to the extreme?
Torque books thrust you into the action-packed world
of sports, vehicles, mystery, and adventure. These books
may include dirt, smoke, fire, and dangerous stunts.
Warning: read at your own risk.

Library of Congress Cataloging-in-Publication Data

Clint, Marc.
 Aztec warriors / by Marc Clint.
     p. cm. -- (Torque: history's greatest warriors)
 Summary: "Engaging images accompany information about Aztec warriors. The combination
of high-interest subject matter and light text is intended for students in grades 3 through
7"--Provided by publisher.
 Includes bibliographical references and index.
 ISBN 978-1-60014-626-8 (hardcover : alk. paper)
 1. Aztecs--Wars--Juvenile literature. 2. Indian weapons--Mexico--Juvenile literature.
3. Aztecs--Juvenile literature. I. Title.
 F1219.76.W37C55 2012
 972--dc22   2011003054

This edition first published in 2012 by Bellwether Media, Inc.

Printed in the United States of America, North Mankato, MN.

080111   1187

Contents

Who Were Aztec Warriors?

Six hundred years ago, the Aztec **empire** ruled much of the land that is now Mexico. The Aztecs were a powerful **civilization**. They showed their might through their fierce warriors. Aztec warriors expanded the empire. They captured enemies for **human sacrifices**. Few armies could stand up to them.

Aztec Fact

Tenochtitlán was the capital city of the Aztec empire. It had many great temples built for the Aztec gods. Prisoners were sacrificed at these temples.

eagle warrior

The deadliest Aztec warriors were called the Shorn Ones. Each warrior had one long braid on the left side of his head. The rest of his head was shaved.

Common people formed the main Aztec army. **Nobles** called *pipiltin* led them into battle. Warriors could earn a higher rank if they captured enemies.

Skilled fighters became eagle warriors or jaguar warriors. Eagle warriors wore feathers and helmets with beaks. They were often used as **scouts**. Jaguar warriors covered their bodies in jaguar skins. They believed the skins gave them the strength of jaguars.

jaguar warrior

Aztec Warrior Training

Aztec boys had to wear their hair short until age 10. After that, their hairstyle depended on their warrior rank.

Every Aztec boy learned basic fighting skills. They practiced with clubs and spears. Boys from noble families received more training. They learned war **tactics** and how to lead armies.

Boys began to join warriors in battle around age 15. They carried weapons and supplies for them. They watched battles and learned from the older warriors.

9

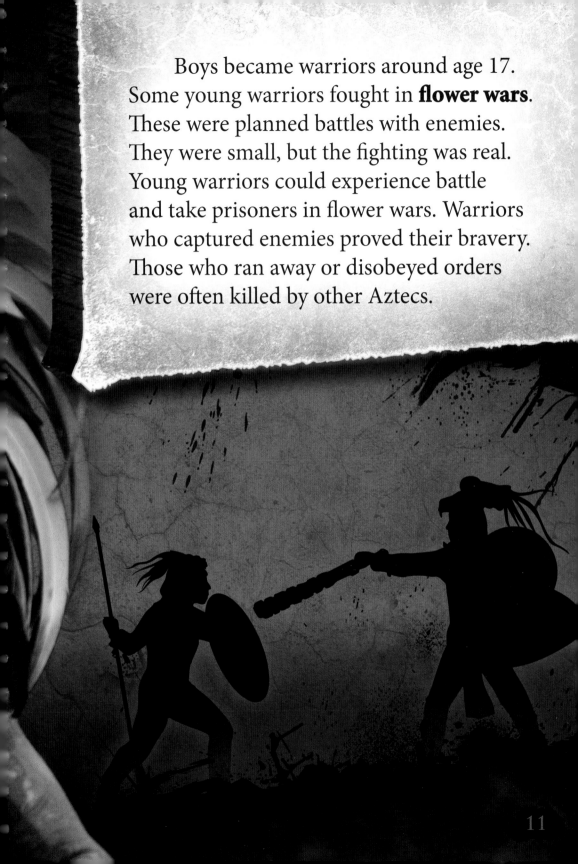

Boys became warriors around age 17. Some young warriors fought in **flower wars**. These were planned battles with enemies. They were small, but the fighting was real. Young warriors could experience battle and take prisoners in flower wars. Warriors who captured enemies proved their bravery. Those who ran away or disobeyed orders were often killed by other Aztecs.

Aztec Warfare: Taking Prisoners

In battle, Aztec warriors tried to capture enemies rather than kill them. An Aztec boy would often take his first prisoner at age 17.

Reasons Aztec Warriors Took Prisoners

- to become adult men

- to move up in military rank

- to move up in social status

- to have human sacrifices for their gods

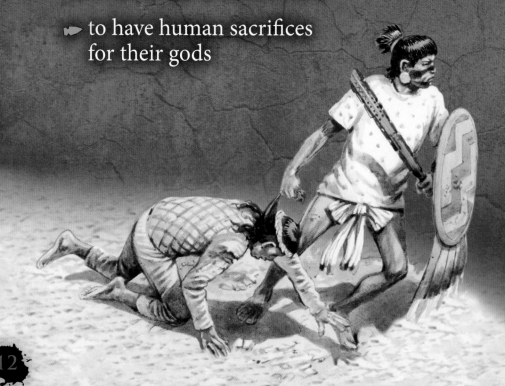

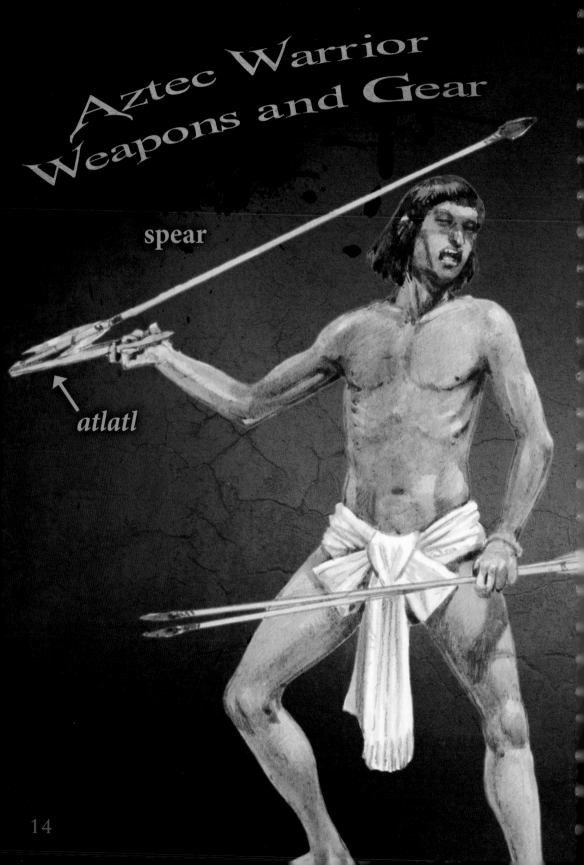

Aztec Warrior
Weapons and Gear

spear

atlatl

Aztec warriors used a variety of weapons in battle. Spears were the most common. They had long wooden shafts and stone or **obsidian** heads. Small spears were used with the *atlatl*, a long-range weapon. The *atlatl* could launch spears very far. Aztecs also used longbows, or *tlahuitolli*, to shoot arrows at enemies.

Clubs and swords were for hand-to-hand combat. Many warriors used clubs to stun enemies. Then they would take them as prisoners. Very skilled warriors carried swords called *maquahuitl*. These swords had many sharp, obsidian blades.

maquahuitl

Warriors needed armor to protect themselves from enemy weapons. *Ichcahuipilli* was armor made of thick cotton. Nobles wore decorated armor. Eagle and jaguar warriors wore helmets that looked like those animals. The *chimalli* was the most common Aztec shield. It was made of wood. Skilled warriors sometimes decorated their shields with feathers and gold.

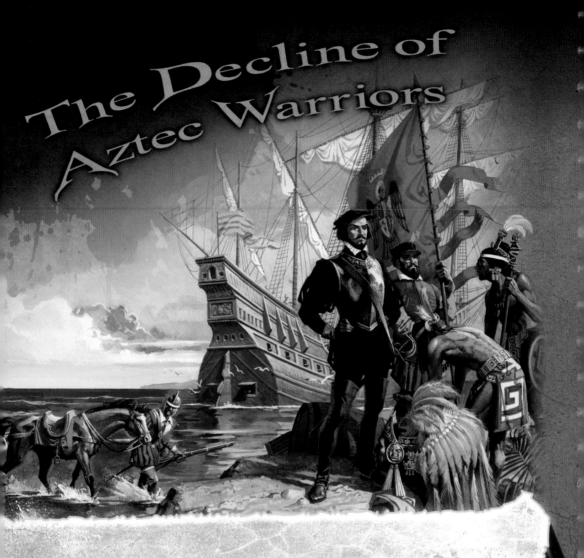

The Decline of Aztec Warriors

In 1502, Montezuma II became the Aztec **emperor**. He wanted to expand the empire. Aztec armies began to conquer many surrounding peoples. In 1519, Spaniard Hernán Cortés and his explorers came to Aztec lands to search for gold.

Montezuma and the Aztecs tried to welcome the Spanish. They were impressed with the Spanish guns, armor, and ships. However, Cortés started a war with the Aztecs because he wanted their gold.

Hernán Cortés

Montezuma II

The Aztec warriors fought bravely, but the Spanish had horses and guns. The Spanish also brought diseases with them from Europe that killed many Aztecs. In 1521, the Spanish conquered Tenochtitlán. The Aztec empire fell apart. Its warriors had fought their final battle.

Aztec Fact

Tenochtitlán later became Mexico City, the current capital of Mexico. Aztec ruins still stand in the city today.

Glossary

civilization—a developed, advanced society

emperor—the leader of an empire

empire—a kingdom made up of many lands

flower wars—small, planned battles between Aztec warriors and their enemies; warriors proved their bravery by capturing prisoners during flower wars.

human sacrifices—humans offered to a god or gods; Aztec warriors captured enemies for Aztec priests to sacrifice to their gods.

nobles—people born into a wealthy or royal family; Aztec nobles led the army.

obsidian—a type of tough glass formed by volcanic activity; obsidian has sharp edges.

scouts—soldiers who search for and watch the enemy before battle

tactics—military strategies

To Learn More

AT THE LIBRARY

Doeden, Matt. *The Aztecs: Life in Tenochtitlán*. Minneapolis, Minn.: Millbrook Press, 2010.

Englar, Mary. *Aztec Warriors*. Mankato, Minn.: Capstone Press, 2008.

Guillain, Charlotte. *Aztec Warriors*. Chicago, Ill.: Raintree, 2010.

ON THE WEB

Learning more about Aztec warriors is as easy as 1, 2, 3.

1. Go to www.factsurfer.com.

2. Enter "Aztec warriors" into the search box.

3. Click the "Surf" button and you will see a list of related Web sites.

With factsurfer.com, finding more information is just a click away.

Index